WELC

ULTIMATE PC GAMING

If a mouse and keyboard have been your main tools throughout your gaming life, or if you're always at the cutting edge of PC technology, then this gaming guide is for you! Dive into the beautiful and captivating worlds of the best games on the planet right now—from the vast lands of *Civilization VI* ready to be conquered, to the competitive maps of *Rocket League*, where goals are waiting to be scored. There is something for everyone! You can also discover some of Steam's hidden gems and the classic games that you need to play right now. There really has never been a better time to be a PC gamer!

CONTENTS

16

44

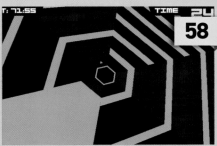

T: 71:55   TIME 24

58

52

EDITOR IN CHIEF
Jon White

EDITOR
Luke Albigés

WRITERS
Steve Ashby, Sam Horti,
Andy Kelly, Drew Sleep,
Mitch Wallace, Josh West

LEAD DESIGNER
Adam Markiewicz

DESIGNERS
Will Shum, Andy Downes

PRODUCTION
Sarah Bankes, Amy Best

COVER IMAGES
Minecraft © 2018 Microsoft Inc.
All rights reserved.
Sid Meier's Civilization VI © 2018
Take-Two Interactive Software, Inc.
All rights reserved.
Hello Neighbor © 2018 tinyBuild. All
rights reserved.
Cuphead © 2018 StudioMDHR
Entertainment Inc.
All rights reserved.
FEZ © 2018 Polytron.
All rights reserved.
Street Fighter V ©
CAPCOM USA Inc.
All rights reserved.

12 REASONS STEAM IS AWESOME

THE BEST FEATURES OF THE LEADING DIGITAL PLATFORM FOR PC GAMING

1 IT'S SAFE AND SECURE

The best thing about Steam is that it's a controlled environment. All available games will work with the launcher, and it's easy enough to get a refund if it turns out your system isn't powerful enough to run a game you've bought. With Family View set up, you can ensure that you're only able to view and launch appropriate content, but you still have easy access to all your favorite games! Family View is the best way for young PC gamers to play, so ask an adult to help set it up for you so you can get the most out of Steam!

2 EVERYTHING YOU LOVE IS IN ONE PLACE

Steam puts your entire gaming library at your fingertips, and what you want to play is never more than a couple of clicks away! While most PC releases are available on Steam, those that aren't—most prominently EA and Blizzard games, which use their own launchers—can usually still be imported into your Steam library and launched from within the client. Having everything available to play just from one launcher is extremely useful, as it means no more thumbing through game boxes or loose discs trying to find what you want to play—just click and go!

THERE ARE MORE GAMES THAN YOU WILL EVER PLAY

> You have plenty of options with Steam's vast catalog of titles, with over 20,000 games available to download and play, while that number grows on a daily basis. Whatever kind of games you like, you're sure to be able to find something to suit your tastes—the software will even do a lot of that for you, recommending and promoting games it thinks you'll like based on what you buy or play most. This can be a great way to discover new games that you can share with your friends, but remember to always check with an adult before buying anything.

3

4 GAMING DOESN'T HAVE TO BE EXPENSIVE

> A lot of people think that gaming is a pricey hobby, but PC players know that couldn't be further from the truth. In addition to the PC versions of big titles often being cheaper than their console counterparts, Steam is renowned for its incredible seasonal sales—when these roll around, you can usually pick up amazing games for mere cents! There are always a ton of great games discounted, with daily and weekly deals, meaning there are always cheap games up for grabs. And on top of that, there are external services like Humble Bundle where you can pick up entire collections of awesome games for just a few bucks. Gaming on a budget has never been easier!

WORKSHOP MAKES GAMES LAST EVEN LONGER

> Mods are a big part of PC gaming, allowing for additions and improvements to games that can add to their longevity. For supported Steam titles, you don't have to brave online file archives or third-party websites to get them—Steam Workshop lets you browse and download content, and user reviews help make sure you get the good stuff!

6

IT'S NOT JUST GAMES

> Creative types will find lots of software to help make amazing things. There are packages available that cater to all skill levels and budgets, so whether you're just a beginner looking to mess around with making your own little adventures in RPGMaker, or a musical expert ready to pen their next hit in something like Samplitude, you'll be able to find what you need for your next exciting project on Steam! Some are even free to use, so why not branch out and try something new?

5

7

BIG PICTURE MODE TURNS IT INTO A CONSOLE

> The addition of Steam's Big Picture mode was a neat new feature. If you typically play PC games on a TV rather than a monitor, this is a great way of streamlining your gaming to make it feel less like a traditional PC environment and more like a console one. You can navigate the menus with the controller, making it easier to swap between games and avoid downtime between fun sessions!

8 GIVE THE GIFT OF GAMING

With all the crazy sales that happen on Steam, you'll often see games you already own and love playing heavily discounted, but that's not a bad thing. Why? Well, if you have friends that also play on PC, you can gift them copies of games directly through Steam—grab a bargain and gift a friend something awesome that you can play together! To make it more exciting, don't tell them you're doing it . . . it's a nice surprise to log in and find a shiny new game waiting for you!

9 WHO DOESN'T LOVE FREE STUFF?

Everybody loves a bargain, right? And what better bargain is there than literally getting something for nothing? Steam has tons of games that can be downloaded and played for free—some of the biggest games on the platform like *Dota 2* and *Team Fortress 2* actually fall into this category. And on top of a wide selection of freebies to add to your library, there are demos and trial versions of some of the biggest games—a great way to try them out before you buy, or just see how well something runs on your PC.

10 IT HAS ITS OWN CONTROLLER

Most PC players swear by the mouse/keyboard control combo due to its versatility and pinpoint accuracy, although Valve's unique Steam controller offers what can be considered the best of both worlds. As well as an analog stick and four-face button, the big draw of this strange-looking pad is the pair of trackpads, offering the precision of a mouse with the simplicity of a stick. It's incredibly versatile and customizable to work perfectly with most Steam games!

THERE'S A HUGE COMMUNITY

11

> Considering it's the biggest platform in all of PC gaming, it should be no surprise to hear that Steam has huge prebuilt communities around all the biggest games. Whether they're sharing cool mods, amazing screenshots, helpful advice, or offers of multiplayer assistance, players are always quick to pool their efforts, and nowhere is it easier to find help for a tricky section of a game, or to find some crazy new way to play that you might never have thought of! Remember to never share your real name or any other personal information such as passwords with anyone you meet or interact with online.

12

CAPTURING THE MOMENT COULDN'T BE EASIER

> One of the best new features of this generation's consoles is the ability to quickly take screenshots of cool moments, but PC players have been enjoying that functionality for years already! With Steam, it's as simple as pressing a key—F12 by default, although you can change this to any key you like—and your picture will be saved to your Steam gallery. From here, you can caption your best images, share them with friends, or simply look back over all the great memories you've had with each of your favorite PC games. Save tons of screenshots!

GET STARTED WITH PC GAMING

PREPARE FOR PC FUN!

MAKE SURE YOUR PC HAS ENOUGH SPACE TO PLAY A GAME

> Your PC has limited storage, and some games take up a lot of it. Before you install a game, check how large it is in the "system requirements" section of its store page, then check what space is on your PC by opening "File Explorer" and clicking "This PC." If you're running out, ask an adult to delete files you don't need.

GET THE RIGHT GADGETS

> To get the most out of your PC you'll need more than just a mouse and keyboard. A gamepad works best for some titles for example. Check out page 56 for the must-haves.

MAKE SURE YOU SAVE YOUR GAMES OFTEN

> If your game crashes and you haven't saved regularly, then you could lose hours of progress. Find out how each game's save system works (look in the "Settings" menu), and save often.

ASK AN ADULT TO HELP YOU GET SET UP

> Setting up your PC for gaming can take a while, and it's easy to make mistakes. Don't go it alone—ask an adult to help you out and you'll be gaming in no time!

DON'T PLAY AGAINST STRANGERS ONLINE

> PC gamers are generally a friendly bunch, but there can be people out to cause trouble, particularly in online multiplayer games. To avoid them, try to only play with a group of friends, or Google family-friendly servers for your game. If anyone harasses you, leave the game and tell an adult.

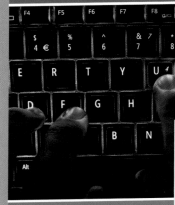

DON'T CLICK ON ANYTHING YOU'RE UNSURE ABOUT

> To avoid getting viruses when setting up your gaming PC, don't click on a link unless you are absolutely sure about where it's taking you. Also, install a free anti-virus program before playing online.

DO YOUR RESEARCH TO BUY THE RIGHT GAMES

> You can't spend money on every game, so it's important to pick ones you'll enjoy. Read reviews and watch YouTube videos of a game before you buy it to get a good idea of the game play.

CHECK WITH AN ADULT BEFORE PAYING FOR ANYTHING

> If you're buying a game with someone else's credit card, then check with them before you check out. If you're spending their money without telling them, they won't be pleased!

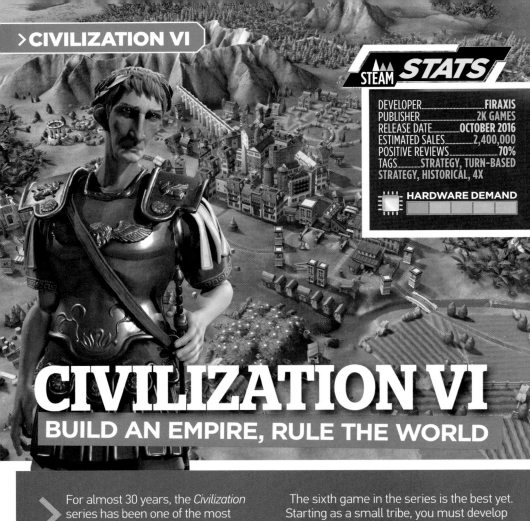

STEAM STATS

DEVELOPER	**FIRAXIS**
PUBLISHER	**2K GAMES**
RELEASE DATE	**OCTOBER 2016**
ESTIMATED SALES	**2,400,000**
POSITIVE REVIEWS	**70%**
TAGS	**STRATEGY, TURN-BASED STRATEGY, HISTORICAL, 4X**

HARDWARE DEMAND

CIVILIZATION VI
BUILD AN EMPIRE, RULE THE WORLD

For almost 30 years, the *Civilization* series has been one of the most popular strategy games on PC. The secret to its success is how addictive it is. When you play it, it's hard to resist just having one more turn. Because that one turn can make a huge difference, whether you declare war on another country or build a monument that is the envy of all your rivals.

The sixth game in the series is the best yet. Starting as a small tribe, you must develop technology and build cities until you become a superpower. Then you have to deal with other world leaders, who will declare war on you at a moment's notice. If you think carefully and use a good strategy, you just might be able to conquer the world and win the game.

TIMELINE

1996

CIVILIZATION II
Civilization II added new units including stealth aircraft, and made managing your empire much easier.

2005

CIVILIZATION IV
This sequel added new ways to achieve victory, including building a starship to take humanity to deep space.

2010

CIVILIZATION V
Civ V was built on a brand-new engine, presenting much better visuals. Combat was also improved a lot.

TOP 5 UNITS

1. SETTLER

The most important unit in any *Civilization* game. These guys will establish a city for you, expanding the reach of your empire. You just have to make sure the city is founded near useful resources.

2. SAMURAI

Fearsome warriors and experts with the blade. These melee fighters will quickly deal with any barbarians trying to raid your cities. But they get less useful when gunpowder is invented.

3. AT CREW

When another nation starts throwing heavy units like tanks at you, you'll need to deploy these antitank troops. They have weak defenses, but their weapons can make short work of the toughest armored units.

4. JET FIGHTER

Dominate the skies with these advanced warfighters. When you have these in the air, it will be difficult for another nation to get the upper hand. But antiair units can also cause them serious problems.

5. PRIVATEER

Rule the seas with these salty dogs. These small ships, crewed by blood-thirsty pirates, will make sure your naval defenses are strong early in the game. Make sure you're the first to research them.

💬 EXPERT COMMENT PHIL SAVAGE Editor, PC Gamer

Human history is a powerful setting, and the *Civilization* series is brilliant for how it manages to build itself around the creation and advancement of technology and culture. Like many other games, the aim is to be the best.

But the context of nation-states competing over a great span of time makes the action feel much more important. *Civilization* brings history to life in a way that no other medium can—letting you negotiate and trade with different world or community leaders, or build the great wonders of the world. It's also cleverly designed, always giving you a new goal or challenge to overcome while creating your perfect world.

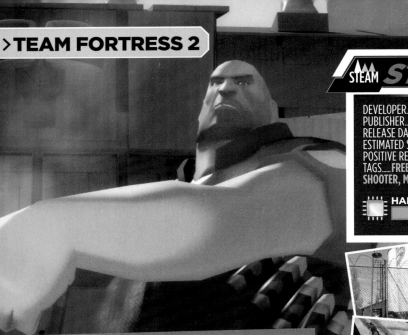

STEAM STATS

DEVELOPER	**VALVE CORPORATION**
PUBLISHER	**VALVE CORPORATION**
RELEASE DATE	**OCTOBER 2007**
ESTIMATED SALES	**43,760,000**
POSITIVE REVIEWS	**93%**
TAGS	**FREE-TO-PLAY, FPS, ACTION, SHOOTER, MULTIPLAYER**

HARDWARE DEMAND

FUN AND FREE TO PLAY
TEAM FORTRESS 2

> As one of the most popular online action games of all time, there's no better place to get acquainted with the thrills and trials of the first-person shooter. *Team Fortress 2* is unquestionably among some of the most fun you can have online; free to play and supported by a steady stream of free updates and content drops, it's the kind of game that helps demonstrate why PC gaming is truly the place to be. With nine distinct classes to choose between, a healthy community behind it to help you understand the basics, and literally hundreds of weapons, hats, and items to collect, *Team Fortress 2* is the kind of game that you will happily spend hours of your time with.

FAVORITE CLASSES

WITH NINE CLASSES TO CHOOSE FROM, HERE ARE OUR FIVE FAVORITES

SPY	MEDIC	SCOUT	HEAVY	ENGINEER
Inherently sneaky, this is your go-to class for deception.	One of the best Support types, no group can be without him.	Your go-to choice when it comes to completing objectives.	If laying down covering fire is your play style, then this is the class for you.	Leave the fighting to the machines and use your smarts.

STEAM STATS

DEVELOPER	CONCERNEDAPE
PUBLISHER	CHUCKLEFISH
RELEASE DATE	FEBRUARY 2016
ESTIMATED SALES	4,000,000
POSITIVE REVIEWS	97%
TAGS	RPG, SIMULATION, PIXEL GRAPHICS, AGRICULTURE, CRAFTING

HARDWARE DEMAND

What a lovely occasion... It's always a joy to visit Stardew Valley.

Governor

STARDEW VALLEY
LIVE OFF THE LAND FOREVER

Who'd have thought planting crops could be so much fun, right? *Stardew Valley* is inspired by *Harvest Moon*, updating the famous farming simulator for the modern era in quite an incredible fashion. Armed with nothing more than a few coins, some rusty old tools, and the help of some super-friendly neighbors, it's your job to renovate an inherited family farm. It may not sound like much, but *Stardew Valley* is one of the best games around; it's easy to pick up and almost impossible to put down, overflowing with charm and character from the start. It's the sort of game that continues to expand and grow the more time you spend on it; in no time you'll have created something to be truly proud of.

HARDEST ACHIEVEMENTS

MYSTERY OF THE STARDROPS	Seven Stardrops are located in *Stardew Valley*. Do you think you can find them all?
CRAFT MASTER	Craft all 94 items in *Stardew Valley* to unlock this resource-draining achievement.
GOURMET CHEF	Start your day watching TV, learn the recipes, then cook every one of them in the game!
PRAIRIE KING	Think you can beat *Journey of the Prairie King*? Good luck. Many try; most fail.
FECTOR'S CHALLENGE	If *Journey of the Prairie King* wasn't tough already, now you must do it without dying!

STEAM STATS

DEVELOPER	CREATIVE ASSEMBLY
PUBLISHER	SEGA
RELEASE DATE	SEPTEMBER 2017
ESTIMATED SALES	500,000
POSITIVE REVIEWS	88%
TAGS	STRATEGY, FANTASY, ACTION

HARDWARE DEMAND

TOTAL WAR: WARHAMMER II

THE MOST EPIC BATTLES ON PC

For years the *Total War* series has been home to some of the most epic battles on PC. While most games are based on real history, this one is set in a fantasy world. It's a game about war and conquest, and lets you take part in battles with thousands of troops filling the screen. And you have to make sure you're using the best strategy to lead your army to victory.

But this involves more than just winning on the battlefield. Between battles you'll use the campaign map to conquer territory, spy on other factions, and use sneaky tactics to weaken your enemy. Strategy games don't get any bigger than this, and the *Warhammer* setting means stuff like magic and demons can exist here, unlike the more historical *Total War* games.

TOP THREE RACES

HIGH ELVES
This ancient, proud race uses smaller groups of elite troops over massive armies.

LIZARDMEN
These creatures are powerful magic users, able to defeat rivals with spells.

SKAVEN
The Skaven only care about themselves, and use surprise attacks to defeat enemies.

STEAM STATS

DEVELOPER	SQUAD
PUBLISHER	SQUAD
RELEASE DATE	APRIL 2015
ESTIMATED SALES	2,000,000
POSITIVE REVIEWS	95%
TAGS	SPACE, SIMULATION, SANDBOX, PHYSICS, SCIENCE

HARDWARE DEMAND

KERBAL SPACE PROGRAM

OUT OF THIS WORLD

Kerbal Space Program blends the silly and the scientific. Your tiny green astronauts may make funny faces as they leave the earth's atmosphere, but they're following a course that strictly obeys the laws of physics. You build a ship out of an endless list of parts, launch it into the air, and see how far it will go. The right formula will land you perfectly on a faraway planet— get it wrong and your Kerbals will splat on the tarmac.

The joy comes in tweaking your ships. Look back on your last flight and you'll realize that you need to add two extra rocket boosters, or rip off two rudders. Through careful thought you'll slowly assemble a perfect rocket ship, and when it all comes together you'll feel like a genius.

TRY THIS!
BOOST YOUR BRAIN WITH MORE SCIENCE GAMES

SPACECHEM
A crafty puzzler that is all about chemicals, and how they're made.

UNIVERSE SANDBOX²
A huge space simulation complete with real-time gravity, climate, and collision systems.

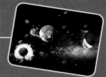

ASTRONEER
Explore the galaxy in a spacesuit and reshape planets as if they were Play-Doh.

THE BEST CLASSIC GAMES

MONKEY ISLAND

> The first two entries in this beloved point-and-click adventure series still hold up today, thanks to their inventive puzzles, fantastic characters, and hilarious jokes. Better yet, both *The Secret of Monkey Island* and *Monkey Island 2: LeChuck's Revenge* got special-edition reissues, giving players the option of the old pixel-art graphics or a new redrawn HD look—you can switch between the two at will!

SENSIBLE WORLD OF SOCCER

> Are modern sports games too complicated for you? This all-time classic couldn't be much simpler, but its basic visuals and controls hide a surprising level of depth. Don't expect up-to-date team rosters, though—the game is more than 20 years old!

X-WING VS. TIE FIGHTER

> This space-combat game is considered by many to be one of the best *Star Wars* tie-ins ever made. While it might lack the spectacle of *Battlefront*, modern games like that arguably wouldn't exist without this multiplayer trailblazer.

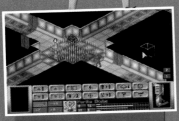

X-COM: UFO DEFENSE

> Defend the earth from alien invasions in this superb strategy game. The many sequels have added new features, but the original's fusion of tactical turn-based missions and in-depth base management is still fantastic fun.

GAROU: MARK OF THE WOLVES

› *Street Fighter III: Third Strike* is undoubtedly one of the best 2-D fighters ever made, but this—SNK's answer to the 1999 Capcom classic—is every bit its equal. A great cast of characters, tight mechanics, and an amazing soundtrack help make this a fan favorite.

THEME HOSPITAL

› Running a hospital is more fun than you might think! It helps that patients here only suffer from silly made-up ailments, such as Bloaty Head, Invisibility, and Slack Tongue. You will need to run a tight clinic to stay on top of the chaos!

SAM & MAX HIT THE ROAD

› This is where it all began for one of gaming's greatest duos! Like the *Monkey Island* games, it's a fantastic comedy point-and-click adventure that set the bar for Telltale's modern episodic games based on the pair of quirky freelance police agents.

ROLLERCOASTER TYCOON

› Theme parks are super fun, but have you ever considered just how much thought, planning, and skill goes into designing and building a roller coaster? Well, you're about to find out! Lay down tracks with steep drops, crazy loops, and intense banked corners in order to excite park visitors—just try not to make your rides *too* crazy or you might make people sick!

STEAM STATS

DEVELOPER.................**DYNAMIC PIXELS**
PUBLISHER.........................**TINYBUILD**
RELEASE DATE...........**DECEMBER 2017**
ESTIMATED SALES......................**36,000**
POSITIVE REVIEWS...........................**63%**
TAGS.........**HORROR, FIRST-PERSON, SINGLEPLAYER, STEALTH, INDIE**

 HARDWARE DEMAND

HELLO NEIGHBOR

NEW KID ON THE BLOCK

Your new neighbor is harboring a horrible secret in his basement, and it's your task to sneak into his home to investigate. The house looks cool, with endless hidden passages and even some roller coaster tracks to navigate as you work your way into its depths.

It's a horror game, but you won't be falling off your chair in shock. It's creepy rather than terrifying, and creates an uneasy atmosphere in which you solve problems to bring you closer to the secret.

This is one for those who like a challenge. The AI will learn your tactics as you go along, and adapt to them. For example, if you keep entering the house through the same window, you might find a bear trap waiting for you. You'll need to think long and hard to outfox your new neighbor!

EXPERT TIPS & TRICKS
FOLLOW THESE AND YOU'LL DO WELL

USE YOUR EARS AS MUCH AS YOUR EYES
Go into a mission with your entire squad showing signs of fatigue, and make it out with no casualties.

ALWAYS BE DISTRACTING
The neighbor is a threat when you don't know where he is. By distracting him you will stay in control.

SWITCH UP YOUR STYLES
If you try the same trick over and over, the neighbor will wise up. Switch up your tactics.

TURN OUT THE LIGHTS
You're harder to spot in the dark. Look out for light switches, or steal a lit bulb.

LOOK THROUGH KEYHOLES
Hold "E" to peer through any keyhole. If the neighbor is there, you should choose another route.

TOP 5 MOMENTS
(WITHOUT SPOILERS!)

THE FIRST TIME YOU'RE CAUGHT

The first time you're caught might give you a scare, but it's an important part of getting better at the game. Learn from your mistakes and you'll be sneaking around in no time.

FEELING CLEVER

This is a game of trial and error, and landing on the right solution to a tricky problem feels great. Just remember to experiment, because some puzzles are not what they seem.

RIDE THE ROLLER COASTER

It's not what you'd expect from a game about sneaking around a house, but who's complaining? Strap yourself in and prepare for one wild ride. Keep an eye on the tracks!

SLEEPING GIANTS

The feeling of hiding from a giant version of the neighbor that peers in through the windows of the house is one to remember. Look out for the cutscene later in the game.

THE TOMATO GOES SPLAT

Splatting a tomato against the neighbor's window will bring him running out, red-faced. In a game that can get fairly complex, it's important to enjoy the simple pleasures.

STEAM STATS

DEVELOPER	**SPORTS INTERACTIVE**
PUBLISHER	**SEGA**
RELEASE DATE	**NOVEMBER 2017**
ESTIMATED SALES	**425,000**
POSITIVE REVIEWS	**61%**
TAGS	**SPORTS, SIMULATION**
	SOCCER, MANAGEMENT

HARDWARE DEMAND

BACK OF THE NET
FOOTBALL MANAGER 2⚽18

Can you lead a little-known team from obscurity all the way to the Champions League? Or build an MLS all-star squad to rival the best sides in the world? It's questions like this that keep players coming back year after year to the *Football Manager* series, and the latest edition offers some new features that keep it feeling fresh.

The Dynamics system is the main one— navigate the media and keep your star players happy off the pitch to find success. Stop your forward from throwing a tantrum and he'll score tons of goals. Anger him and you'll have a team-wide crisis on your hands. Add improved AI, a sleeker interface, and a reworked match engine, and you have one of the best entries in the series to date.

THE NEW FEATURES OF FM18

DYNAMICS
Keep your promises to players and you'll have harmony in the dressing room.

MEDICAL CENTER
The new treatment facility tells you why players are injured.

SCOUTING SYSTEM
Scouting gets its own budget, and it's easier to see which players will shine.

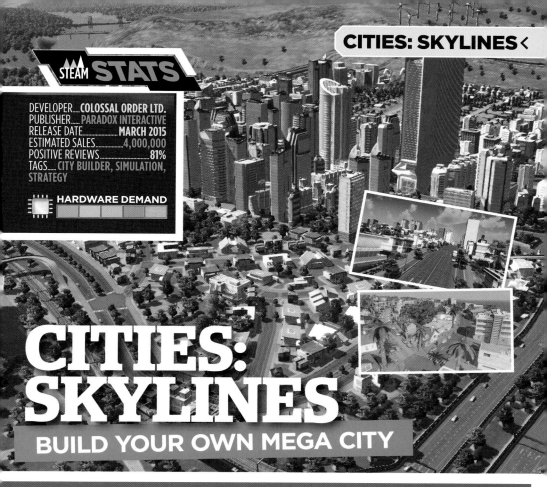

STEAM STATS

DEVELOPER.....**COLOSSAL ORDER LTD.**
PUBLISHER.....**PARADOX INTERACTIVE**
RELEASE DATE.................**MARCH 2015**
ESTIMATED SALES.............**4,000,000**
POSITIVE REVIEWS.....................**81%**
TAGS......**CITY BUILDER, SIMULATION, STRATEGY**

HARDWARE DEMAND

CITIES: SKYLINES
BUILD YOUR OWN MEGA CITY

Do you have what it takes to run a city? *Cities: Skylines* puts you in charge of everything from laying out the roads to making sure there are enough fire trucks and police cars to deal with emergencies. You start on an empty field, building a small network of roads to get your city started. Then over time it rapidly grows, from a small village to a metropolis like New York City.

But your life as the mayor won't be easy. There are lots of ways for things to go wrong, including the threat of a natural disaster. Earthquakes, tornadoes, and fires are just a few of the problems you'll have to deal with. Not to mention providing enough houses and jobs for your citizens. It's a stressful job, but the joy of seeing your city grow and flourish makes it worth it.

TOP THREE MODS
THE BEST CHANGES FOR YOUR GAME

FLIGHT SIMULATOR
Take control of one of the planes flying above your city and enjoy the view.

FIRST-PERSON CAMERA
Walk around your amazing city from the perspective of one of your loyal citizens.

STARGATE
Add a futuristic public transport system. Buses are so old-fashioned, man.

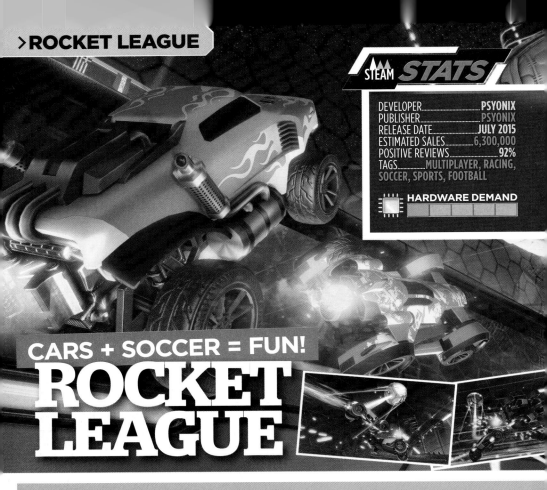

STEAM STATS

DEVELOPER	**PSYONIX**
PUBLISHER	**PSYONIX**
RELEASE DATE	**JULY 2015**
ESTIMATED SALES	**6,300,000**
POSITIVE REVIEWS	**92%**
TAGS	**MULTIPLAYER, RACING, SOCCER, SPORTS, FOOTBALL**

HARDWARE DEMAND

CARS + SOCCER = FUN!
ROCKET LEAGUE

If rocket-powered cars hitting a giant ball around a futuristic arena to score goals doesn't sound awesome, we don't know what does! This crazy game mixes soccer with driving to create one of the coolest sports we've ever seen. You and your team need to work together to push, hit, and generally shove the huge ball into the opposition's goal, while they try to do the same to you. Driving on walls, soaring through the air, and exploding other cars is all allowed, so prepare for the fastest-moving game of soccer you've ever seen! Other modes mix things up, adding a basketball variant, or throwing in power-ups that do crazy things like grow a giant boxing glove from your car to punch the ball away. Madness!

COOLEST ACHIEVEMENTS

BRAG TO YOUR FRIENDS IF YOU UNLOCK THESE CHALLENGES!

 THE STREAK
WIN TEN GAMES IN A ROW ACROSS ANY MODE.

 HELEN'S PRIDE
SCORE SIX GOALS IN A SINGLE GAME.

 STILL A SHOW-OFF
SCORE A GOAL WHILE REVERSING YOUR CAR.

 SKY HIGH
SCORE AN AERIAL GOAL IN A MATCH.

 CHAMPION
WIN THE SEASON CHAMPIONSHIP.

CUPHEAD

STAR IN YOUR OWN CARTOON!

Jump into an amazing cartoon world, and beat the toughest bosses you'll ever face! This side-scrolling platformer sees you facing off against huge, screen-filling baddies that want nothing more than to send Cuphead and his pal, Mugman, drifting off the top of the screen. To defeat them, you'll need to shoot magical projectiles out of Cuphead's finger as you dodge their endless attacks. As the screen fills with cartoon explosions, and the action ramps up, you'll need every shred of gaming skill to triumph! Of course, you can always just sit back and enjoy the visual treat on screen. The entire game was painstakingly hand-drawn and hand-painted, just like a real cartoon from the 1930s, and the result is spectacular—it really will feel like you're in a cartoon TV show!

BEST BOSSES
THREE OF THE COOLEST BADDIES TO BEAT!

BARONESS VON BON BON
This angry boss isn't as sweet as she looks! Watch out for her delicious but deadly attacks.

CARLA MARIA
Don't be fooled— this mermaid has electric eels that will try to shock you!

SALLY STAGEPLAY
This actress just wants to complete her play, and she will do anything she can to finish it.

STEAM STATS

DEVELOPER ..... **FRONTIER DEVELOPMENTS**
PUBLISHER ..... **FRONTIER DEVELOPMENTS**
RELEASE DATE ..... **NOVEMBER 2016**
ESTIMATED SALES **1,000,000**
POSITIVE REVIEWS **89%**
TAGS ..... **SIMULATION, BUILDING, MANAGEMENT, SANDBOX, STRATEGY**

HARDWARE DEMAND

PLANET COASTER

BUILD YOUR DREAM THEME PARK

> Theme parks are never as good as you imagine they will be. That's why a game like *Planet Coaster* is so much fun. Build your own coaster park empire, letting your imagination run wild as you put crazy rides together piece by piece. *Planet Coaster* is designed around ease of use, ensuring that every player can become a master designer and sculptor in just minutes. Take your rides underground or up into the sky; sit back and watch as an authentic physics system ensures your rides (and their passengers!) have realistic reactions—even if your designs don't—then take delight in sharing your creations with other park builders across the globe.

BEST DLC

SPOOKY PACK
Get this DLC if you want to create a park that is positively frightful.

KNIGHT RIDER K.I.T.T. CONSTRUCTION KIT
Bring the *Knight Rider* legend to life. You might need to ask your parents—they'll understand.

BACK TO THE FUTURE TIME MACHINE CONSTRUCTION KIT
Give your park a *Back to the Future* themed overhaul, complete with DeLorean!

DEVELOPER.................THEKLA, INC.
PUBLISHER..................THEKLA, INC.
RELEASE DATE............JANUARY 2016
ESTIMATED SALES............600,000
POSITIVE REVIEWS................84%
TAGS.............PUZZLE, EXPLORATION,
FIRST-PERSON, SINGLEPLAYER,
COLORFUL

 HARDWARE DEMAND

THE WITNESS

CHALLENGING AND BEAUTIFUL PUZZLE DESIGN

Prepare to have your persistence put to the test in *The Witness*. It's a beautiful and challenging puzzle game, cast out across a gorgeous island, masterfully crafted and impossibly inventive. What's great about *The Witness* is that it's aware of its own difficulty, and there's always something else to steal away your attention should you find yourself butting heads with a seemingly impossible lateral-thinking test. If you get stuck, it won't punish you; instead, you can move on to one of the other dozens of locations in the world, and try a different intelligent puzzle. There are more than 500 in the game, and none are fillers; each explores different ideas and themes. It will make you feel like a mastermind should you make it to the end.

SIMILAR GAMES

REALMYST
The legend updated—as difficult, obtuse, and fun today as it was back in 1993.

OBDUCTION
A sci-fi adventure set in a strange, surreal world. Have a game guide handy.

THE VANISHING OF ETHAN CARTER
A beautiful first-person narrative adventure, focused on story over puzzle-solving.

THE BEST NON-STEAM GAMES

AWESOME OUTSIDERS FOR YOUR STEAM LIBRARY

MINECRAFT
Even better on PC!

> The insanely popular survival blockbuster (pun very much intended) started out on PC, and is still the best version of the game to this day—it looks better, it controls better, it's just better! Here's why . . .

MODS
PC players get to expand their game by installing mods, extra programs that alter the game in all kinds of ways. Some of these might be simple—such as being able to see chests highlighted through terrain—while others completely change the game, adding new mechanics, items, features, and modes. *Minecraft*'s potential as a game is vast, but with mods on top, it's *infinite*.

CONTROLS

The flexibility of a mouse/keyboard setup makes it the best input solution for a game like this—it's much quicker and easier to navigate, gather, build, and fight like this than it is with a controller, and it's hard to go back once you've tried mining and crafting with a mouse and keyboard! If you'd rather use a pad, there are ways to get that working on PC, too.

SHADERS

These are like mods, just for *Minecraft*'s graphics rather than its gameplay. Shaders alter and improve the game's lighting, varying in hue and technique from shader to shader, so some will work better in certain maps and modes than others. The downside of shaders is that they can be extremely memory-intensive, so you'll need a powerful PC if you want *Minecraft* to look its best!

CROSS-PLAY

Despite all these improvements, you can still play with friends online across a variety of platforms—with the Better Together update, players on PC, mobile, Xbox One, and Switch can build, break, and battle together as one big happy family! Mods aren't available for the console versions, though, so you might have to disable some to play together.

OVERWATCH

> What do you get when you mix Disney Pixar movies with tons of super-fun first-person action? Blizzard's mega-popular online hero shooter, *Overwatch*, that's what. With regular updates like fresh maps, characters, and holiday modes, this awesome multiplayer game is showing no signs of slowing down. Assume the role of a gorilla scientist, a cyborg ninja, or even a junkyard demolitionist as you compete in tense team matches that award you with valuable loot boxes.

1

CONTROL POINT UNLOCKS IN: 15

ATTACK

3%

500 / 500

WORLD OF WARCRAFT 2

> Still considered to be the most popular and successful MMO of all time, *World of Warcraft* was first released way back in 2004. Seven expansion packs and over a decade later, the game is still going strong. Millions of people still log in every day, so if you create a new character and jump in as a newbie, you'll have plenty of trusty adventurers at your side as you explore the mysterious land of Azeroth. The developers even recently added classic servers that run the game in retro style.

DESTINY 2

3

> Take on the role of a Guardian, a powerful Earth protector who you can customize. Go to various planets to stop the evil Dominus Ghaul, all while earning new armor and weapons as you complete missions. The best thing about *Destiny 2* is that you're playing it alongside thousands of other gamers, and when you get your Guardian to a high enough level, you can start going on exciting raids with friends.

ROBLOX

4

> Released in 2005, *Roblox* is a free, massively multiplayer online game that is actually a bunch of games, and a handy tool for making them. There are thousands of unique titles, and they're all made by fellow gamers. The choice is yours: deliver pizzas, be Spider-Man, play hide-and-seek with SpongeBob, go to high school, adopt kids . . . the options are endless, and there are always new *Roblox* games coming out.

5 LEAGUE OF LEGENDS

> *League of Legends* is a multiplayer online battle arena popular with pro eSports players. Gamers choose Champions from a roster of fighters, tanks, mages, marksmen, assassins, and support characters before joining other warriors to fight on the battlefield. The objective? Infiltrate the other team's base, and take down its Nexus before they do the same to you. Winning comes down to good teamwork and tons of strategy.

THE SIMS 4   6

> The fourth game in the long-running life-simulation series allows players to create, guide, and interact with in-game characters known as Sims. Keep them happy with food, showers, bathroom visits, and naps. Once you've got those basic skills mastered, you can build houses for your digital people, get jobs, have them adopt pets or play virtual reality video games, and even say "Awww!" as they fall in love. It's a whole lot like real life, only in weird video-game form.

7

STAR WARS: BATTLEFRONT II

> **Building** on 2015's next-gen *Star Wars: Battlefront* game, this sequel gives gamers the option of conquering a story-driven campaign or jumping into the returning action-packed online multiplayer mode. Choose from a host of classic heroes like Chewbacca, Luke Skywalker, Yoda, and even villains like Darth Maul or Darth Vader. Then pilot awesome *Star Wars* vehicles like AT-RTs, X-wings, or the iconic *Millennium Falcon*.

8

HEARTHSTONE

> A free-to-play, virtual trading-card game based on *World of Warcraft*, *Hearthstone* is a lot like *Pokémon* and *Magic: The Gathering*. Open packs, get rares and legendaries, then take your loot out onto the card battlefield where you can cast damaging spells and summon dangerous beasts against skilled online opponents. It's all about building the perfect deck of cards to take down your adversaries, and collecting more cards as you play is tons of fun. Easy to learn and challenging to master, you'll be playing this one for a while.

WORLD OF TANKS

> What happens when you get a bunch of turrets and treads together for an all-out video-game war? *World of Tanks*—a massively multiplayer online combat simulator where it's every gamer for themselves. Choose an armored fighting machine, and battle against other players in chaotic free-for-alls across large maps. As you win, earn rewards to upgrade your fleet and unlock new vehicles.

9

10

FIFA 18

> Sports games keep getting more realistic, and *FIFA 18* is no exception. The ultimate soccer simulation allows gamers to play as their favorite soccer athletes, who look and move exactly like they do in real life. Build your own team, play through the dramatic story mode, or take the ball online to sweep, strike, and defend against thousands of fellow worldwide fans.

ADDING GAMES TO STEAM
All your favorites in one place!

⚙ Open up the Steam client on your computer and look toward the top of the program. Above the "Store" and "Library" icons you should see a few other options like "Steam," "View," "Friends," and "Help." Click on "Games" and in the menu that appears, click on "Activate a Product on Steam."

⚙ A window will pop up that explains the process of registering your game with Steam, followed by a box where you can enter letters and numbers. This is where you'll type in your digital game code or whatever kind of code your physical game disc came packaged with (usually found inside the case or printed on the instruction manual).

⚙ Once you've entered the game code and pressed "Next," your game is officially registered and you can now launch it from inside your Steam library.

STEAM STATS

DEVELOPER..........**AIRSHIP SYNDICATE**
PUBLISHER...................**THQ NORDIC**
RELEASE DATE.............**OCTOBER 2017**
ESTIMATED SALES..................**65,000**
POSITIVE REVIEWS....................**89%**
TAGS.....**RPG, TURN-BASED COMBAT, INDIE, JRPG, SINGLEPLAYER**

HARDWARE DEMAND

BATTLE CHASERS: NIGHTWAR

CLASSIC DUNGEON CRAWLING ACTION

From the mind of artist Joe Madureira comes the revival of *Battle Chasers*, the beloved comic book series that earned itself a cult following in the nineties. *Nightwar* is an JRPG inspired by the genre greats, but distinctly modern in its execution. That means you should expect deep dungeon diving action and challenging turn-based combat that doesn't frustrate; beautiful randomly generated dungeons that are keen to throw new surprises in your direction; and a deep crafting system designed to bring a degree of customization to each of the six available heroes! *Battle Chasers: Nightwar* is a compelling JRPG that respects your time, expertly straddling the line between nostalgic action and a fresh new feel.

TOUGHEST ACHIEVEMENTS

CAN YOU COMPLETE THESE TRICKY CHALLENGES?

BIG GAME HUNTER	NO PARLEY	FISH WATCHING	A FANTASY, FINALIZED
FILL EVERY SINGLE PAGE IN THE BESTIARY.	FIND THE SECRET PIRATE CAPTAIN AND DEFEAT HIM.	TURN YOUR HAND TO FISHING AND COMPLETE THE FISHIARY.	FINISH THE GAME ALL OVER AGAIN ON NG+ MODE.

STEAM STATS

DEVELOPER..**GEARS FOR BREAKFAST**
PUBLISHER...**GEARS FOR BREAKFAST**
RELEASE DATE............**NOVEMBER 2017**
ESTIMATED SALES.....................62,181
POSITIVE REVIEWS....................98%
TAGS **3D PLATFORMER, CUTE, INDIE, FEMALE PROTAGONIST, ADVENTURE**

HARDWARE DEMAND

A HAT IN TIME

THE CUTEST PLATFORMER EVER!

Explore strange new worlds as the heroic Hat Girl in this platform adventure! Our heroine travels through the universe saving the planets she visits from the evil Mustache Girl—yes, the baddie in this story is a girl with facial hair! When her spaceship crashes, Hat Girl has to explore five amazing worlds to collect Time Pieces, which will power up her ship again. She'll also find new hats that give her abilities, which will help her fight the bosses that she meets along the way.

The coolest part of the game, though, is the lands you get to explore with Hat Girl. There are tons of awesome ways to get around each level, whether it's zooming along zip-lines, leaping across gaps, or swinging from poles. And as you explore each world, you'll find tons of hidden secrets!

COOLEST HATS
GET SPECIAL POWERS WITH THESE ACCESSORIES!

KID'S HAT
Find your way to the next point of interest with this one!

SPRINT HAT
Wear the sprint hat and you can run super fast.

DWELLER'S MASK
You can see through the Dweller's eyes with this mask and materialize objects.

STEAM STATS

DEVELOPER	TOBYFOX
PUBLISHER	TOBYFOX
RELEASE DATE	SEPTEMBER 2015
ESTIMATED SALES	2,990,000
POSITIVE REVIEWS	95%

TAGS.....GREAT SOUNDTRACK, STORY RICH, CHOICES MATTER, FUNNY, RPG

HARDWARE DEMAND

UNDERTALE
A CUT ABOVE THE REST

Undertale is a game that every PC gamer should play. Don't be put off by its old-school looks, because this is one of the best RPGs you'll ever get your hands on. Its humor is its best feature: you will genuinely laugh out loud at its jokes, and enjoy talking to all of its cast of wacky characters, including a skeleton that loves to drink ketchup.

But it's not a silly game by any means. Behind the jokes is a clever story that you play a key role in shaping through your decisions. There's multiple endings, and you can get through the game without hurting a soul. Or you can go all-out combat and leave a trail of bodies in your wake. The choice is yours—there's no wrong way to play it!

TIPS & TRICKS

PLAY THROUGH IT MORE THAN ONCE
Your first run will take six hours or so, but you won't regret playing through again to learn all of its secrets.

DON'T READ ANY SPOILERS!
For most games, researching before you buy is a good idea. But here, that spoils the fun. Go in blind!

TALK YOUR WAY OUT OF TROUBLE
Killing monsters might be fun, but it will make the game difficult. Hit "Act" during combat to talk to them instead.

GO PACIFIST FOR THE BEST REWARDS
Keeping everyone alive means more story. So keep your sword in its sheath if you want to see everything.

STOCK UP ON BISICLES
You can buy Bisicles in Snowdin, one of the early towns. Stock up, because they're the best healing items.

TOP 5 CHARACTERS

2. PAPYRUS

The younger brother of Sans has a massive ego, but also a kind heart. He's a complex character that boasts one minute and spares your life the next. As funny as Sans, too.

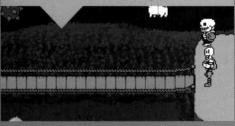

1. SANS

A laid-back skeleton that cracks some of the game's best jokes, as well as puns that are so bad you can't help but laugh. In combat, he's an unstoppable whirlwind.

3. THE MAIN CHARACTER

Even the name of the main character is a secret, so let's keep you guessing! You build up a real emotional attachment to her, and her decisions shape the game world.

4. TORIEL

One of the first characters you'll meet in *Undertale*'s mysterious world. She has a kind heart, and she'll give you your first gut-wrenching decision of the game. Have the tissues handy.

> I am TORIEL, caretaker of the RUINS.

5. UNDYNE

An inspirational, heroic character who's not afraid to lay down her life to save others. She's tough and determined in combat and hilarious when she wants to be.

STEAM STATS

DEVELOPER	**DODGE ROLL**
PUBLISHER	**DEVOLVER DIGITAL**
RELEASE DATE	**APRIL 2016**
ESTIMATED SALES	847,000
POSITIVE REVIEWS	**92%**
TAGS	**BULLET HELL, PIXEL, LOOT, GRAPHICS, DUNGEON CRAWLER**

HARDWARE DEMAND

NUMBER ONE WITH A GUN!

ENTER THE GUNGEON

Enter the Gungeon is all about its weapons. There are a whopping 200 of them, each sillier than the last. When you're bored with a magic lamp that sends out a genie to punch enemies, you can pick up a Rad Gun, which fires faces wearing sunglasses and increases damage with each reload.

You blast your way through difficult dungeon floors, picking up upgrades and abilities while defeating weird and wonderful bosses to reach the next stage. Every room is a challenge, with bullets flying anywhere, and the bosses are some of the hardest enemies you'll face with a control pad. One bad reload or missed dodge roll can be deadly, so pick your weapon and bring your A game.

TRY THIS!
THREE GAMES HARDER THAN ENTER THE GUNGEON

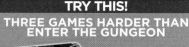

CUPHEAD
A retro-style shooter that will leave you tearing your hair out.

SUPER MEAT BOY
Guide a cube of meat through tough, twisting, and treacherous levels.

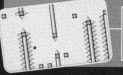

I WANNA BE THE GUY
A platformer that exists to cause you pain. Beating it is a top achievement.

STEAM STATS

DEVELOPER..................................**CAPCOM**
PUBLISHER....................................**CAPCOM**
RELEASE DATE............**FEBRUARY 2016**
ESTIMATED SALES..................**335,000**
POSITIVE REVIEWS.........................**51%**
TAGS.........**FIGHTING, MULTIPLAYER, COMPETITIVE, 2D FIGHTER**

 HARDWARE DEMAND

STREET FIGHTER V
BUTTON MASHERS BEWARE

Street Fighter V could be the game that gets you into the fighting genre. Yes, there's lots of flashy combos and plenty of deep tactics for longtime fans, but it focuses on strikes, positioning, and timing, which makes it welcoming to newbies. Combo timing is easier than ever, and the special move system gives everyone a chance.

Each fighter has a "V-Skill" that they can use at any time, and doing so builds up charge for their "V-Trigger." These are powerful moves but, unlike the special moves of past *Street Fighters*, won't take off half your health bar in one hit. That means you can stay in a fight if your enemy gets on top. Controls are tight and to cap it off, the game looks like a work of art.

WHO TO USE

BEST CHARACTERS FOR BEGINNERS

RYU
The famous fireball flinger is the perfect all-rounder to help start your *Street Fighter* journey.

CHUN-LI
A kick specialist with a powerful V-Trigger move that boosts all of her strikes.

NASH
Previously a clone of the more famous Guile, Nash comes into his own in *SFV*.

HIDDEN STEAM GAMES

WINDOSILL

> Even if you've played tons of video games, chances are you've never seen anything quite like *Windosill*. The idea is simple: Click on objects and animals to solve interesting puzzles. The coolest part is that every creature and trinket does something totally different, so a big part of the fun is just seeing what wacky event happens next.

APPLE JACK 1&2

> Usually you get in trouble for playing with your food, but never in this weird 2-D sidescrolling platformer. Play as a tiny dude with a green apple for a head who runs, jumps, and throws washing machines.

RISK OF RAIN

> This tough 2-D action game combines retro 8-bit graphics, four-player online co-op, and perma-death, which means that once you die, it's game over. Take down randomly generated baddies and explore a strange planet.

STEPHEN'S SAUSAGE ROLL

> One part cooking simulator and one part mind-bending riddle, this bizarre top-down puzzle game has you figuring out how to cook sausage links without burning them. Simple but extremely challenging.

CONTRADICTION

> Newer video games are kind of like movies, but this live-action murder mystery takes it to a whole other level. Interview real people and figure out who's lying and who is telling the truth.

SUPER FANCY PANTS ADVENTURE

> School notebook doodles come to life in this fast-paced 2-D platformer. Armed with a trusty fountain pen and some fancy parkour moves, you guide your hand-drawn hero through dozens of colorful levels.

RIVALS OF AETHER

> The elements of air, earth, water, and fire collide in this 16-bit style platform fighting game. Enter the fray as one of several different animal fighters including a lion, a raccoon, and an orca.

SAMOROST 3

> The odd name of this beautiful point-and-click game basically means "cool stuff made out of wood," which makes a lot of sense once you start exploring all of its surreal, living environments. The third entry in the adventure series has you guiding a plucky space gnome (along with his magical flute) across the universe in search of many puzzles to solve and strange creatures to meet.

STEAM **STATS**

DEVELOPER	CHUCKLEFISH
PUBLISHER	CHUCKLEFISH
RELEASE DATE	JULY 2016
ESTIMATED SALES	3,000,000
POSITIVE REVIEWS	90%
TAGS	SANDBOX, ADVENTURE, SURVIVAL, INDIE, CRAFTING

HARDWARE DEMAND

TERRARIA IN SPACE!
STARBOUND

Get ready to explore the farthest reaches of the galaxy! Don't be deceived by its simple 2-D graphics—*Starbound* is incredibly vast and complex, with a universe of cool stuff to discover. You'll soon find a planet to call home and can get to work building a base of operations, befriending the locals and fending off any hostile alien creatures. But once you're done with a planet, you can just hop into your spaceship and blast off for another, where you'll find all kinds of new adventures and discoveries waiting for you. It's like having a galaxy of interconnected *Terraria* saves, each with their own biomes, resources, and hazards, and you can even go exploring with friends thanks to the cooperative multiplayer mode, too!

HARDEST ACHIEVEMENTS
CAN YOU COMPLETE THESE TRICKY CHALLENGES?

DESTROYER OF WORLDS	**ARMOR AFICIONADO**	**BUG FREE**	**THEM BONES**	**MINT CONDITION**
MOVE A PLANET'S WORTH OF BLOCKS.	COLLECT 210 UNIQUE PIECES OF ARMOR.	CATCH 42 UNIQUE BUGS.	UNEARTH 55 UNIQUE FOSSILS.	COLLECT AT LEAST 50 UNIQUE ACTION FIGURES.

STEAM STATS

DEVELOPER................GLUMBERLAND
PUBLISHER.................DOUBLE FINE
RELEASE DATE...................2018
ESTIMATED SALES................N/A
POSITIVE REVIEWS..............N/A
TAGS.........SIMULATION, RPG, INDIE,
ADVENTURE, CUTE

HARDWARE DEMAND

OOBLETS

GROW YOUR OWN FRIENDS!

If you like *Pokémon, Animal Crossing*, or *Harvest Moon*, then you're going to fall in love with *Ooblets*! It combines elements of those three popular series to create a super-cute and original experience—new companions are first grown like crops, then raised like friends, and can be battled like Pokémon. Both your character and home can be fully customized as you wish, as can the town around it as you progress through the game. Improve your farm for a better harvest; open a shop to sell goods that you no longer need; join a club that is specific to your favorite type of ooblet . . . this colorful world can be grown into whatever you want it to be, the perfect place for you and your team of ooblet friends to play!

MEET THE OOBLETS
INTRODUCING SOME OF OUR FAVORITE CREATURES SO FAR . . .

CHICKADINGDING

FLEEBLE

FRIPP

GLOOPYLONGLEGS

WIGGLEWIP

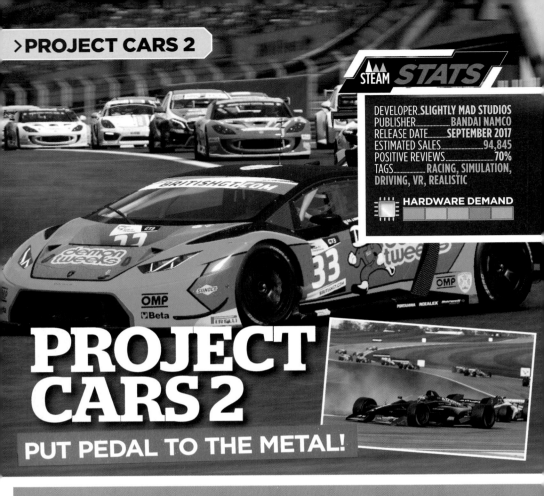

STEAM STATS

DEVELOPER	**SLIGHTLY MAD STUDIOS**
PUBLISHER	**BANDAI NAMCO**
RELEASE DATE	**SEPTEMBER 2017**
ESTIMATED SALES	**94,845**
POSITIVE REVIEWS	**70%**
TAGS	**RACING, SIMULATION, DRIVING, VR, REALISTIC**

HARDWARE DEMAND

PROJECT CARS 2

PUT PEDAL TO THE METAL!

Feel the speed with this super-fast racer! If you've ever wondered how it feels to drive a supercar like a Lamborghini or McLaren, then this is the game for you. *Project Cars 2* offers an incredibly realistic driving experience, with some of the best-looking cars that you've ever seen in a video game. Whether you're skidding around a rallycross track in a muddy car or sitting behind the wheel of a powerful V8 vehicle, you'll feel like you're really in control. What's more, if you've got a VR headset, you can use it to play the game for a more immersive experience. Put it on, slip on some headphones, and you'll feel like you really are right there in the driver's seat, zooming around corners at hundreds of miles per hour.

COOLEST CARS

THE SWEETEST RIDES YOU CAN TAKE FOR A SPIN

LAMBORGHINI HURACÁN SUPER TROFEO
With 611 horsepower, this car is one of the most powerful in the game.

LAFERRARI
A hybrid engine produces enough power to take this from 0-125 mi/h in under seven seconds!

ACURA NSX
This hybrid combines electric and gasoline motors to enhance performance.

MCLAREN 720S
The design of this McLaren was inspired by the body of a great white shark, making it incredibly slick.

STEAM STATS

DEVELOPER.................TEAM CHERRY
PUBLISHER..................TEAM CHERRY
RELEASE DATE.........FEBRUARY 2017
ESTIMATED SALES..............602,000
POSITIVE REVIEWS....................93%
TAGS..............METROIDVANIA, GREAT
SOUNDTRACK, DIFFICULT, PLATFORMER

HARDWARE DEMAND

HOLLOW KNIGHT

GET LOST IN ADVENTURE

Plenty of video games have tried to pick up the torch and carry on blazing a trail for the *Metroid* and *Castlevania* franchises, but few have done so quite as confidently as *Hollow Knight*. One of the finest releases of 2017, this debut release from developer Team Cherry is an incredible sidescrolling action game that pushes you to explore a unique gothic dungeon—crawling with monsters and mysteries to find, fight, and conquer. The world is expansive and open, designed to be returned to over and over again as you unlock new abilities and discover new items to break through its interconnected highways; *Hollow Knight* is a wonderfully designed game that never fails to delight, challenge, and test your ability. Do yourself a favor and play this modern gem.

SIMILAR GAMES

AXIOM VERGE
Dark, dank, and decidedly old school; a classic Metroidvania experience.

CAVE STORY
A beautiful weave of old influences and fresh new mechanics.

ORI AND THE BLIND FOREST
Heartfelt and challenging until its end, a must play.

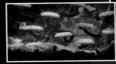

SEASONS AFTER FALL
A hearty blend of puzzles and platforming drive this fun adventure.

BEST 8 VR GAMES

GAMES BROUGHT TO LIFE

AUDIOSHIELD

> This intense arcade game turns your own music against you. Red and blue spheres shoot toward you in time with the music, and you have to bounce them back with the red and blue pads on your hands. Choose a slow song and it's pretty easy. But import some heavy metal or fast dubstep and you'll really work up a sweat trying to keep up with your tunes.

FRUIT NINJA VR

> The addictive mobile game is now available in VR. Swing your samurai swords and slice the fruit as it's thrown at you. Speed and accuracy is the key to stacking up those combos and scoring major points.

KEEP TALKING AND NOBODY EXPLODES

> Essentially, one player is trapped in a room with a ticking time bomb, and the other player has the manual to tell them how to defuse it. This intense cooperative game will really test you and your friends' communication skills.

SUPERHOT

> Time only moves in this cool FPS when you move. A power you can use to dodge between bullets as they fire through the air, then take your enemies out with melee weapons, guns, or just your fists.

REZ INFINITE

This arcade shooter is set inside a computer. A virus has infected the system and it's your job to fly through a series of colorful levels, using a laser to drive the virus away. But the coolest thing about *Rez Infinite* is how your attacks make the music, so it is just like you are creating your own soundtrack.

JOB SIMULATOR

Working in a burger restaurant or an office really doesn't sound fun, but this crazy game is no real-life simulation. You will make a mess and annoy customers as you throw stuff around your virtual workplace.

EAGLE FLIGHT

Experience what it's like to fly like a bird in this VR game. You take control of a majestic eagle, gliding across the city of Paris. And thanks to the power of virtual reality, you really feel like you're flying.

STAR TREK: BRIDGE CREW

Become the captain of the famous starship *Enterprise*, commanding your crew (played by your friends) to attack enemies and keep the ship from blowing up. It's just like being in the *Star Trek* movies.

>FTL: FASTER THAN LIGHT

PUT YOUR MIND TO THE TEST
FTL: FASTER THAN LIGHT

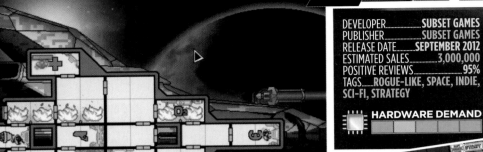

Have you ever pictured yourself as the captain of a starship, exploring the deepest reaches of the galaxy? Well, it's harder than it looks, folks, we'll tell you that right now! *FTL: Faster Than Light* is a challenging strategy game in which you are tasked with guiding your crew and ship through dangerous sectors of space, navigating difficult combat situations against strange alien species and daring rogue humans. You'll need to use the power of conversation to talk your way out of diplomatic fiascos, and do your best to manage resources in a series of increasingly perilous situations. If your crew gets killed or your ship obliterated it's game over, but that shouldn't deter you from giving this game a try. *FTL: Faster Than Light* is one of the most entertaining games you are likely to find on Steam.

SIMILAR GAMES

TEST YOUR SKILLS WITH THESE OTHER STRATEGY GAMES

STAR COMMAND GALAXIES
Become a captain, recruit your crew, and explore space.

SPACE ROGUE
Explore new worlds and engage in tense ship-to-ship combat.

CONVOY
This tactical combat game takes *FTL*-style gameplay to the desert.

RENOWNED EXPLORERS
Tactical and tough, this indie hit is a very rewarding challenge.

STEAM STATS

DEVELOPER	**MOON STUDIOS**
PUBLISHER	**MICROSOFT GAME STUDIOS**
RELEASE DATE	**MARCH 2015**
ESTIMATED SALES	**740,000**
POSITIVE REVIEWS	**95%**
TAGS	**GREAT SOUNDTRACK, ATMOSPHERIC, PLATFORMER, 2D**

HARDWARE DEMAND

ORI & THE BLIND FOREST
A BEAUTIFUL ADVENTURE

Few video games are able to achieve a level of consistent excellence quite as confidently as *Ori & the Blind Forest*. It's set across a gorgeous, sumptuous hand-painted world that Moon Studios has crafted into one of the best action-platformers of the decade. While you can encounter a little difficulty—progress through the interconnected world gated by the skills and ability upgrades you unlock—you'll find yourself enchanted by the story and soundtrack, the tight controls, and engaging puzzles. Meticulously well designed, constantly engaging, and somber right through to the very end (it's okay if it makes you cry toward the end, we sure did), *Ori & the Blind Forest* is a must play for everybody with a PC capable of running it.

SIMILAR GAMES
CHECK OUT THESE PLATFORMERS

HOLLOW KNIGHT
An epic action-adventure; one of the year's best!

CHILD OF LIGHT
A beautiful fantasy adventure with fun strategy battles.

OWLBOY
Story-driven adventure game with absolutely gorgeous graphics.

DUST: AN ELYSIAN TALE
A hand-painted world with a really deep story and combat.

STEAM STATS

DEVELOPER	FIRAXIS
PUBLISHER	2K GAMES
RELEASE DATE	FEBRUARY 2017
ESTIMATED SALES	1,800,000
POSITIVE REVIEWS	80%
TAGS	STRATEGY, TURN-BASED, TACTICAL, ALIENS, SCI-FI

HARDWARE DEMAND

XCOM 2
TAKE BACK THE PLANET

> Take the fight to the alien overlords, engage in tactical combat, and find yourself crashing up against a brutal difficulty curve. If one of your soldiers dies, then they are out of the game for good. But you shouldn't let that deter you, because *XCOM 2* is king when it comes to turn-based strategy. Your mission is to take back earth, traveling to take on a variety of enemy types and challenging situations. *XCOM 2* is a flexible, fun, and personable game, made all the more engaging as it lets you build up a customizable squad and tailor the experience to your personal tastes through a variety of weapons and abilities. *XCOM 2* is difficult, but it's also an amazing strategy game that has no equal.

RAREST ACHIEVEMENTS
LOOKING FOR A REAL CHALLENGE?

WEARY WARRIORS	WHO NEEDS TYGAN?	THE FEW AND THE PROUD	HEAVY METAL	IMMORTAL COMMANDER
Go into a mission with your entire squad of soldiers showing signs of fatigue, and make it out successfully with no casualties.	Get through the stupidly hard last mission of the game using only conventional human gear.	Somehow beat the game on the tough Commander+ difficulty, but do it without ever increasing the size of your squad.	Find and/or develop all of the heavy weapons within the game and kill an enemy with each of them.	Legendary difficulty is difficult enough at the best of times, but this requires you to overthrow all the aliens in one playthrough.

TOP 5 TIPS

1. USE STEALTH

XCOM 2 presents an environment in which the humans are on the back foot. While it can be easy to rush into encounters, the best tip we can offer is to take every mission as it comes. Use stealth, set up ambushes, and try to take as many enemies off the board before it kicks off.

2. CUSTOMIZE YOUR SQUAD

One of the coolest things to do in *XCOM 2* is to personalize your entire squad, giving each of them a custom name, weaponry, and abilities. Better still, base each of them around your friends and family to really increase the tension throughout every mission.

3. IT'S OKAY TO FAIL

XCOM 2 is a really punishing game and you shouldn't be afraid to fail. Part of the fun is embracing the perma-death aspect; if one of your soldiers gets killed, don't reload; keep pushing forward. The loss will only make you think more tactically in future missions.

4. RESOURCE MANAGEMENT

Once the difficulty starts ramping up, you'll want to be aware of where your resources are going. It's possible to fail if you don't manage them, so get your priorities right early on and follow through on your research trees.

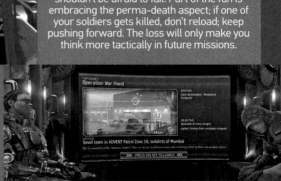

5. EXPERIMENT WITH DIFFICULTIES

The difficulty scale can be imposing in *XCOM 2* and there's nothing wrong with paring it back if you find yourself getting stuck. That said, there's a lot of fun to be found in the crushing challenge of Impossible and Iron Man modes.

💬 EXPERT COMMENT — JOSH WEST
Deputy editor, gamesTM magazine

There aren't many games on the market quite like *XCOM 2*. It's a challenging strategy game that will test everything from your situational awareness to your research management skills and tactical ability. You'll want to customize your squad so that they reflect that of your friends and then take great joy in leading them into dangerous battles. The thrill is found in the surmounting challenge, making each victory feel hard earned and worth the pain. Given its difficulty and the huge breadth of options and opportunities available to you, expect *XCOM 2* to represent real value for money—this isn't a game you'll blast through in a weekend, that I can promise you right now!

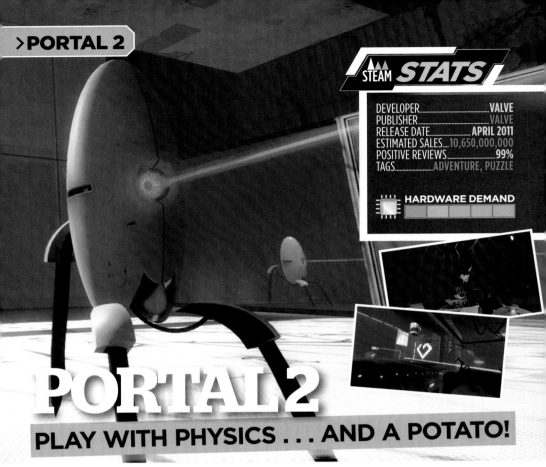

STEAM **STATS**

DEVELOPER	**VALVE**
PUBLISHER	VALVE
RELEASE DATE	**APRIL 2011**
ESTIMATED SALES	10,650,000,000
POSITIVE REVIEWS	**99%**
TAGS	ADVENTURE, PUZZLE

HARDWARE DEMAND

PORTAL 2
PLAY WITH PHYSICS . . . AND A POTATO!

Not only one of the best sequels of all time but one of the greatest games to ever grace a gaming machine period, *Portal 2* is a bona fide classic. Trapped like a rat in a maze, you must navigate the ruined hallways of the Aperture Science facility using your trusty portal gun to get from A to B—or is that from blue to orange? That

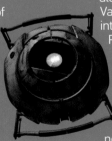

alone should get you interested but Valve keeps on upping the ante, introducing new ways to use your Portal Gun, taking you to places that you wouldn't even think possible before topping things off with a climax that's out of this world. *Portal 2* is a masterclass in game design, story, and creativity. Do yourself a favor and install it now—you will not regret it.

LAB RAT
SOME OF THE TESTS YOU'LL BE RUNNING

 FALLING FORWARD
HARNESS MOMENTUM FROM FALLING TO LEAP FORWARD GREAT DISTANCES.

 IT'S ALIVE
YOU CAN MAKE A POTATO SENTIENT. NOTE: IT MAY WANT TO KILL YOU.

 TARGET PRACTICE
HELP TO NOT CALIBRATE SENTRY BOTS' AIM BY SNEAKING AROUND THEM INSTEAD.

 BOUNCE BACK
USE REPULSION GEL TO REACH NEW HEIGHTS, AND USE TURRETS AS BOUNCY BALLS.

 PORTAL PALS
CONTROL A ROBOT AND ROPE IN A FRIEND TO SOLVE CO-OP PUZZLES.

STEAM STATS

DEVELOPER	MOSSMOUTH
PUBLISHER	MOSSMOUTH
RELEASE DATE	AUGUST 2013
ESTIMATED SALES	940,000,000
POSITIVE REVIEWS	77%
TAGS	INDIE, PLATFORMER, ROGUELIKE

HARDWARE DEMAND

THE WALLS ARE SHIFTING
SPELUNKY

Do you possess an adventurer's spirit? A thirst for treasure? A desire to save damsels, dogs, or . . . sloths? Then look no further than getting your hands dirty in *Spelunky*'s caves. Don't let that cartoonish Indiana Jones-like explorer and those adorable graphics fool you, though, *Spelunky* is tough. It's the type of roguelike that you'll keep bashing your head against just to gain an inch of progress; as you explore the subterranean labyrinth you'll encounter everything from dart traps and spike pits, to snakes and yetis. No two levels are the same, and don't even think for a moment that you can just take your time and ease your way through its levels: if you take too long you'll be doggedly chased by a deadly ghost. Steel yourself, explorer: you're going to need your wits for this excursion.

ADVENTURERS-HO!
THERE'S LOTS OF PLAYABLE CHARACTERS, BUT THESE ARE THE BEST

SPELUNKY GUY	Your regular old vanilla avatar. Kind of like Indiana Jones.	
VAN HELSING	Gentleman, vampire slayer, and owner of fantastic mutton chops.	
LOST GIRL	Must've wandered off from a school trip . . . poor thing.	
ROBOT	You'd think its metal body would help protect it . . . it really doesn't.	
MEAT BOY	Wait a second . . . haven't we seen this guy before?	

STEAM ACCESSORIES

ULTIMATE KIT FOR A PC GAMER

A PROPER HEADSET

By blocking out external noise, gaming headsets make you feel a part of the Steam game you're playing. Plus, they normally come with microphones so you can talk to your teammates, which is vital for working together.

GAMING MOUSE

A bog-standard mouse is fine for most games, but a gaming mouse is much better. It's more comfortable to use, it has extra buttons to program, and higher sensitivity, so your clicks are more accurate.

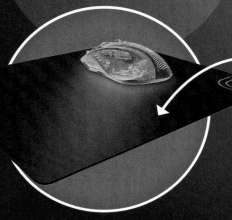

GAMING MOUSE MAT

What's the point in having a good mouse if you're running it over an uneven surface? Gaming mouse mats are completely flat and smooth, giving you more control of your on-screen movements.

A RELIABLE GAMEPAD

Mouse and keyboard control is great, but for some Steam games (like platformers), you'll do better with a gamepad. Pick one that you're used to and make sure it will work on PC. Wired pads are best.

A GAMING KEYBOARD

As a PC gamer you'll likely be hammering your keys, so you'll want a keyboard that can take the punishment. Gaming keyboards are reliable, have extra keys, and won't buckle under heavy use. Plus, they look cool!

AN EXTERNAL HARD DRIVE

For PCs with less storage an external hard drive can work wonders. For best performance, install games on these drives and transfer them one by one to your PC's main drive via Steam before you play.

GAMING CHAIRS

Games are best enjoyed when you're sitting comfortably. So trade in that rickety office chair for a gaming seat if you can. Sink into the leather and lose yourself in another world.

HIGH-QUALITY SPEAKERS

Headsets are great, but sometimes you want your ears out in the open, such as when you have friends over. For those times, decent speakers can really help you enjoy your Steam games.

STEAM STATS

DEVELOPER............. **TERRY CAVANAGH**
PUBLISHER............. **TERRY CAVANAGH**
RELEASE DATE........... **NOVEMBER 2012**
ESTIMATED SALES.............**1,000,000**
POSITIVE REVIEWS.....................**97%**
TAGS............**DIFFICULT, INDIE, GREAT SOUNDTRACK**

HARDWARE DEMAND

SUPER HEXAGON

ARE YOU READY FOR A CHALLENGE?

> Developed by one man, *Super Hexagon* seems like it is simple on the surface, but is actually one of the hardest games on PC. You control a small triangle, and must guide it through a series of hexagons that are constantly moving toward you. That sounds easy, but the speed of the hexagons and the way the path constantly changes makes it almost unbearably difficult.

But when you start making progress, from lasting 3 seconds to 20, you find yourself becoming addicted to it. But to make things even harder, the longer that you manage to hold out, the faster and more intense the hexagons become. You'll need the reactions of a fighter jet pilot to last more than a minute, but it can be done if you stick with it. Give this one a try, and you might be surprised by how much you love it.

TOP THREE HARD GAMES

SUPER MEAT BOY
This platformer stars a boy made of meat who has to make his way through levels filled with spikes, traps, and sawblades.

CANABALT
A man dashes through a city as it's destroyed by alien invaders. You have to keep running, and one mistake means game over.

CUPHEAD
Based on old cartoons, this side-scrolling shooter features tricky bosses to take down, and some really cool animated visuals.

STEAM STATS

DEVELOPER...**BRACE YOURSELF GAMES**
PUBLISHER.................**BRACE YOURSELF GAMES, KLEI ENTERTAINMENT**
RELEASE DATE............**APRIL 2015**
ESTIMATED SALES...............**926,000**
POSITIVE REVIEWS...................**97%**
TAGS........**RHYTHM, ROGUELIKE, GREAT SOUNDTRACK, PIXEL GRAPHICS**

 HARDWARE DEMAND

CRYPT OF THE NECRODANCER
SLAYING MONSTERS TO THE BEAT

Half dungeon crawler, half disco, *Crypt of the NecroDancer* is a step ahead of most roguelikes. Don't be fooled by its simple looks—this is a complicated game where you build up combos by moving in time with the funky soundtrack. Get the timing right and the gravel beneath your feet turns into a dance floor, and you receive more gold for every monster you slay.

Swerving between attacks to the rhythm feels great. After a few hours you'll have it down to an art, and as you improve you'll gain new weapons that help you progress into the dungeon with every life. Best of all, you can team up with a friend in local co-op and use your own MP3s as a soundtrack.

TRY THIS!

THREE MORE GREAT GAMES THAT COMBINE MUSIC AND COMBAT

THUMPER
Guide a space beetle through a series of psychedelic levels. A brutal challenge.

REZ INFINITE
This legendary shooter blends combat, colors, and music into two hours of pure gaming heaven.

ONE FINGER DEATH PUNCH
Kick waves of enemies with one-button kung fu moves.

GAMER CHALLENGE

CHECK YOUR GAMING CRED

01 What is the name of Hat Girl's archnemesis in *A Hat in Time*?

02 True or false: The *Civilization* series has been going for almost 30 years.

03 In *Stardew Valley*, you are renovating what?

04 In *Team Fortress 2*, what is the go-to class for completing objectives and escaping firefights?

05 What color are the astronauts in *Kerbel Space Program*?

06 In *Football Manager 2018*, which new feature allows you to keep track of injured players?

07 What other sporting mode does *Rocket League* have to offer?

08 True or false: *Cuphead* was completely hand-drawn.

09 True or false: *Minecraft* started on a console.

10 How many weapons are there in *Enter the Gungeon*?

11 What is the name of the rat-like race in *Total War: Warhammer II*?

12 True or false: *World of Warcraft* was first released in 2004?

13 What is the name of the virtual trading-card game based on *WoW*?

14 How many players can play *Risk of Rain*?

15 In which game do you guide a space gnome?

HOW DID YOU SCORE?

 0-5 Gaming noob: You need to step it up!

 6-10 Casual gamer: You could do better!

 11-14 Hardcore gamer: You really know your stuff!

 15 Gaming god: You totally rock!

ANSWERS 01: MUSTACHE GIRL 02: TRUE 03: FAMILY FARM 04: SCOUT 05: GREEN 06: MEDICAL CENTER 07: BASKETBALL 08: TRUE 09: FALSE 10: 200 11: SKAVEN 12: TRUE 13: HEARTHSTONE 14: FOUR 15: SAMOROST 3

ROLLERCOASTER TYCOON
MANAGE YOUR OWN THEME PARK

> FIRST RELEASED March 1999 **> COPIES SOLD** 4,000,000 **> DEVELOPER** Chris Sawyer Productions

Everyone loves a theme park, but what if you could build your own? *RollerCoaster Tycoon* lets you design your own roller coasters and rides, but there are other things to consider too. Are there enough toilets in your park? And if people aren't spending enough money on soda, you can always put extra salt in the french fries. This simulation is deep, and you even have to make sure your rides are exciting enough. If the roller coaster doesn't make them puke, you'll have to get more creative with your design. Remember, the more they scream, the more successful your park will be.

END GAME

THE STANLEY PARABLE
The game with 19 endings

An oldie but a goodie. Obey the commands of the game's brilliant narrator or stick your tongue out and do your own thing. There's a whopping 19 endings, so be unpredictable and try to see them all.